THROUGH THE DECADES
THE 1930s
THE HOBBIT
eureka!
BY SARA GREEN

Eureka! books turn real stories into unforgettable experiences. This nonfiction imprint sparks curiosity, encourages critical thinking, and engages middle-grade readers. *Eureka!* books empower young minds to explore the stories of the real world, one fascinating fact at a time. Unravel the power of knowledge and lifelong learning with *Eureka!*

This edition first published in 2026 by Bellwether Media, Inc.

Library of Congress Cataloging-in-Publication Data

LC record for The 1930s available at: https://lccn.loc.gov/2025028070

Editor: Rebecca Sabelko Designer: Andrea Schneider

Printed in the United States of America, North Mankato, MN.

TABLE OF CONTENTS

WELCOME TO THE 1930s!

It is 1932 and times are tough. A girl trudges to her uncle's house after school. Her family moved in with him after her dad lost his job. She misses her old house where she had her own bedroom, toys, and a closet filled with nice clothes. Now, she shares a small bedroom with her younger brothers. There is little money for new toys, and her clothes have been mended countless times.

That evening, the girl helps her mother set the table for dinner. Like most nights, they are having beans, bread, and gravy. Nobody complains. Everyone is grateful to have something to eat. The girl cannot wait until her uncle's garden yields fresh carrots and spinach! She glances at her dad's empty chair. She misses him, but her mother says things will improve once he finds work.

Life is not all bad, though. The girl enjoys swimming in the pond and playing kick the can with her friends. Every night, the family listens to radio programs. *The Shadow* is her favorite! The 1930s are filled with ups and downs!

MENDING SOCKS

WHAT HAPPENED IN THE 1930s?

The **Great Depression** defined the 1930s. The 1920s, known as the Roaring Twenties, was a time of prosperity for many Americans. But after the stock market crashed in 1929, the United States fell into a depression. Banks failed and millions of people lost their savings, jobs, and more. The economic slump would last through the decade. A severe drought in parts of the South Central region led to more hardships. This environmental disaster is known as the Dust Bowl. Farmers could no longer grow crops, and many of them lost their farms.

Economic instability led to political chaos in other parts of the world. The rise of **authoritarianism** in Germany and Italy along with other political events set the stage for World War II, forever changing the course of history.

The 1930s also saw glimmers of hope. Government programs known as the New Deal provided relief to people. They would eventually help pull the country out of the Depression. Meanwhile, people learned to be thrifty and self-reliant. They found entertainment in movies, art, and music. Radio and television technologies advanced. Life during the Depression would significantly shape the decades to come.

GROWING CITIES

New York City was the largest city in the U.S. in 1930. It had a population of 6,930,446. Chicago was second largest, with a population of 3,376,438. Philadelphia's population came in third at 1,950,961.

New York City construction workers in 1932

HOW MUCH?

1 GALLON GAS
20 CENTS (1930)
19 CENTS (1939)

THE NEW YORK TIMES
(Greater New York)
2 CENTS (1930) | 3 CENTS (1939)

1 QUART MILK
14 CENTS (1931)
11 CENTS (1939)

A DOZEN EGGS
35 CENTS (1930)
28 CENTS (1939)

FIRST-CLASS STAMP
2 CENTS (1930)
3 CENTS (1939)

HERSHEY BAR
5 CENTS

LOAF OF BREAD
9 CENTS

HISTORY

UNITED STATES HISTORY

The Great Depression affected the lives of millions of Americans. Many people suffered great hardships, including the loss of jobs, homes, and possessions. Communities of makeshift shacks built by unhoused families sprang up around the country. These communities were called Hoovervilles after President Herbert Hoover, whom many blamed for their hardships.

The 1930s also saw major achievements. Government programs that are still used today, such as Social Security, were developed. The Empire State Building in New York City was completed in 1931. It was the tallest building in the world at the time and stood as a symbol of American progress.

In 1932, aviator Amelia Earhart became the first woman to fly solo across the Atlantic Ocean. She broke new ground in women's rights and inspired women and girls across the nation to pursue their dreams.

HOOVERVILLE IN SEATTLE, WASHINGTON

THE EMPIRE STATE BUILDING

AMELIA EARHART

GOLDEN GATE BRIDGE

Construction of the Golden Gate Bridge began in 1933. The bridge opened on May 27, 1937, for Pedestrian Day. Around 200,000 people paid 25 cents each to walk, run, dance, and even roller-skate across the bridge. The bridge was opened to vehicles the next day. It was both the longest and tallest suspension bridge in the world at the time!

Pedestrian Day on the Golden Gate Bridge

Dust Bowl refugees

MIGRANT WORKERS

The Dust Bowl forced millions of people to abandon their farms. Many of them moved to California, seeking better opportunities. The migrants were nicknamed Okies because many of them came from Oklahoma. Wealthy landowners often took advantage of Okies, paying them low wages for hard work. Many Okies lived in **squalor** in makeshift camps.

HINDENBURG DISASTER

The *Hindenburg* was a luxurious rigid airship used to carry passengers over long distances. On May 6, 1937, the *Hindenburg* burst into flames while attempting to land in New Jersey. The accident killed 35 of the 97 people on board. The disaster led to widespread public distrust in airships and brought an end to airship transportation.

O SAY CAN YOU SEE

On March 3, 1931, "The Star-Spangled Banner" was adopted as the U.S. national anthem.

UNITED STATES POLITICS

The country was in crisis at the onset of the 1930s. In 1930, Congress passed the Smoot-Hawley **Tariff** Act. It placed high taxes on products imported to the U.S. The act aimed to protect U.S. manufacturing and farm production. However, it sparked a global trade war when other nations hit back with their own tariffs. World trade dropped by more than 66 percent after the act was passed and worsened the Great Depression.

President Herbert Hoover

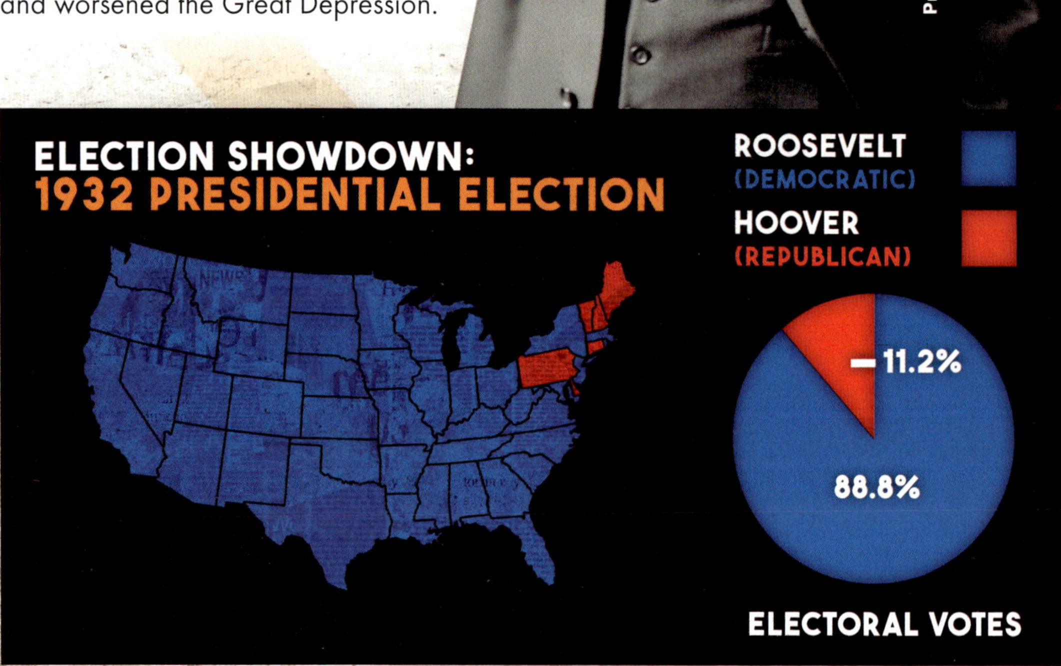

President Hoover started a few public relief programs such as the Emergency Relief and Construction Act. However, Hoover did not want people to rely on the government. He believed people could regain prosperity through hard work combined with voluntary aid from the business community. Still, hard times wore on. Many Americans believed President Hoover was uncaring. They lost confidence in him and were ready for a change.

In 1932, Franklin D. Roosevelt, the Democratic governor of New York, ran for president. He pledged to relieve people's suffering and lift the economy out of the Depression. His message of hope inspired millions of Americans. Roosevelt won the election in a landslide! In 1935, Congress passed the National Labor Relations Act, which helped **labor unions** achieve major gains.

FIRESIDE CHATS

President Roosevelt delivered a series of radio addresses called fireside chats between 1933 and 1944. The president addressed issues of public concern in an informal, relaxed manner to reassure the American people and inform them about government actions.

DEMONSTRATORS UNHAPPY WITH PRESIDENT HOOVER

WORKERS VOTING FOR UNION BOARD MEMBERS

PRESIDENT ROOSEVELT DELIVERING A FIRESIDE CHAT

SPOTLIGHT ON:

THE NEW DEAL

Shortly after becoming president in 1933, Roosevelt called Congress into a three-month session. They created new programs to give relief to American citizens and help the economy recover. These programs were called the New Deal. One of the first New Deal programs was called the Emergency Banking Act. It aimed to stabilize the banking system and restore public confidence. The Act closed banks and the Federal Reserve for four days. During the "bank holiday," examiners checked banks' financial health. When the banks reopened, the panic had mostly subsided. People began to deposit money in banks again.

Other early New Deal programs included the Civilian Conservation Corps and the Public Works Administration. They put many unemployed people to work improving parks, planting trees, and building hospitals, schools, and dams. The Works Progress Administration (WPA) was formed in 1935. It employed more than 8 million people across the country. WPA employees built 650,000 miles (1,046,074 kilometers) of roads, 800 airports, and 75,000 bridges. The Social Security Act, passed in 1935, gave financial security to retired workers 65 and older. Millions of Americans continue to rely on Social Security today!

MAKING HEADLINES

"Recovery Has Arrived, Says President"

–*Santa Fe New Mexican*, September 6, 1935

"ROOSEVELT TO MAKE JOBS FOR 3,500,000 NOW ON RELIEF; PUSHES HIS SOCIAL PROGRAM"

–*THE NEW YORK TIMES*, JANUARY 5, 1935

WHO'S WHO?

"Washington Gives New Deal Huge Confidence Vote; '130' Defeated"

–*Washington New Dealer*, November 12, 1938

WORKS OF ART

The WPA Federal Art Project paid artists to create pieces for public parks and buildings. A huge amount of art was produced, including 2,566 murals, over 100,000 paintings, and around 17,700 sculptures!

FRANKLIN DELANO ROOSEVELT

ROLE:

President of the U.S. (1933 to 1945)

KNOWN FOR:

Roosevelt quickly began a set of government programs called the New Deal after becoming president. The New Deal helped the country recover from the Great Depression.

WORLD HISTORY

The economic downturn of the 1930s caused widespread poverty and social unrest in many countries. This led to the rise of authoritarian leaders, territorial expansion, and political turmoil. New dictatorships arose in Central America. Japan invaded China, and Italy expanded into Ethiopia.

Germany also experienced widespread civil unrest in the aftermath of World War I. Economic and political chaos led to Adolf Hitler's rise to power. In defiance of the **Treaty of Versailles**, Hitler remilitarized Germany and moved troops into the Rhineland. **Appeasement** and other efforts to de-escalate global conflicts largely failed, paving the way for the onset of World War II.

PROTESTERS AGAINST THE ITALIAN INVASION OF ETHIOPIA

JAPANESE SOLDIERS IN THE SECOND SINO-JAPANESE WAR

Anastasio Somoza García, dictator of Nicaragua

GERMAN TROOPS ENTERING THE RHINELAND

SPANISH CIVIL WAR

In July 1936, Nationalist troops led by General Francisco Franco revolted against the democratically elected government of Spain. This uprising escalated into a civil war that lasted for three years, ending with a Nationalist victory. Franco ruled as dictator and head of state from 1939 until his death in 1975.

General Francisco Franco

KRISTALLNACHT

On the night of November 9, 1938, the Nazi Party launched a violent attack against Jews throughout Germany, parts of Austria, and what was then Czechoslovakia. For 48 hours, mobs set fire to synagogues and destroyed thousands of homes and businesses. Shattered glass littered the streets. Nearly 100 Jewish people were killed. Nazis arrested around 30,000 Jewish men and sent them to Nazi concentration camps. This attack came to be known as *Kristallnacht*, or the "Night of Broken Glass."

JAPAN'S INVASION OF CHINA

In 1931, Japan invaded Manchuria, a region in northeast China, to expand its territory and obtain natural resources. This event eventually led to the onset of the Second Sino-Japanese War in 1937. In December, Nanjing, China's capital, fell to Japanese forces. They committed horrific acts against Chinese citizens and left the city in ruins.

SPOTLIGHT ON:

INVASION OF POLAND

Hitler's appointment as chancellor of Germany in 1933 put the Nazis in a position of power. They immediately established a police state, banned all other political parties, and implemented polices aimed at "racial purification." The Nazis were also determined to expand German territory.

On September 1, 1939, Nazi troops invaded Poland in an unprovoked attack, triggering the start of World War II. The Nazis implemented a strategy called Blitzkrieg, or "lightning war." It relied on speed, force, and the element of surprise to achieve a quick victory. German soldiers, airplanes, and tanks crossed the Polish border from the north, south, and west. Their rapid attacks quickly overwhelmed Polish defenses. Great Britain and France demanded that Hitler pull out of Poland. When he refused, the two countries declared war on Germany on September 3. German forces continued advancing into Polish territory, killing civilians and burning cities.

The Soviet Union invaded Poland as part of a German-Soviet **nonaggression pact** on September 17. The Germans and Soviets greatly outnumbered the Polish armed forces. On September 28, the Polish surrendered in Warsaw, Poland's capital. Poland was then divided between Germany and the Soviet Union.

MAKING HEADLINES

"War Rages on Polish Front"

—*The Deseret News*, September 1, 1939

"WAR: GERMAN WARPLANES BOMB POLAND'S CAPITAL; NAZIS ANNEX DANZIG; HEAVY BORDER FIGHTING"

—*THE DETROIT FREE PRESS*, SEPTEMBER 1, 1939

WHO'S WHO?

Hitler and Nazi soldiers in Danzig, Poland

ADOLF HITLER

ROLE:
Leader of Nazi Party and chancellor and eventual dictator of Germany (1933 to 1945)

KNOWN FOR:
Hitler triggered the start of World War II in 1939, invaded many countries, and led the Nazis in the murder of around 6 million Jewish people in what is known as the Holocaust.

SOCIAL CHANGES

The role of women shifted during the Depression. Domestic work, teaching, and other jobs labeled "women's work" were less affected by the economic downturn. Women entered the workforce in great numbers to help their families survive the hard times. For the first time in U.S. history, women made up around a quarter of the workforce. Women also found work through New Deal programs. The Pack Horse Library Project sent librarians into rural areas to bring books, magazines, and newspapers to people who otherwise would not have access to them. The librarians traveled by horseback when necessary!

First Lady Eleanor Roosevelt

AN INSPIRING FIRST LADY

Eleanor Roosevelt was the First Lady of the U.S. from 1933 to 1945. She was a tireless advocate for social and economic justice and a champion for women, people living in poverty, and people of color.

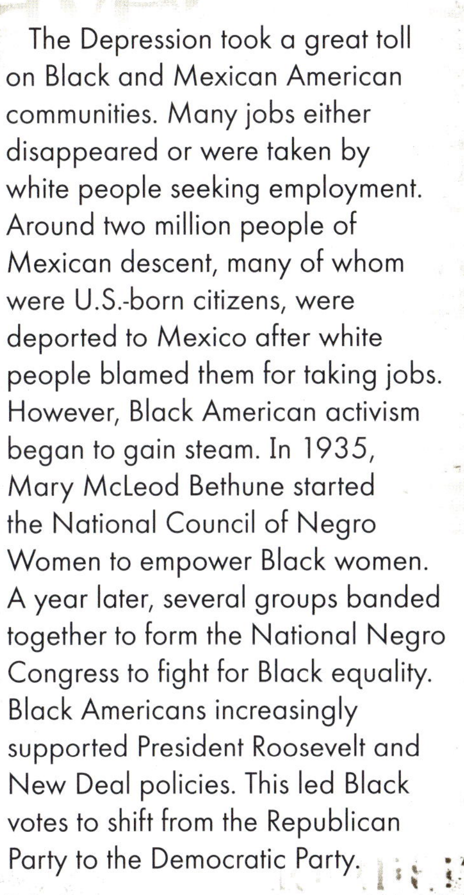

The Depression took a great toll on Black and Mexican American communities. Many jobs either disappeared or were taken by white people seeking employment. Around two million people of Mexican descent, many of whom were U.S.-born citizens, were deported to Mexico after white people blamed them for taking jobs. However, Black American activism began to gain steam. In 1935, Mary McLeod Bethune started the National Council of Negro Women to empower Black women. A year later, several groups banded together to form the National Negro Congress to fight for Black equality. Black Americans increasingly supported President Roosevelt and New Deal policies. This led Black votes to shift from the Republican Party to the Democratic Party.

WOMEN TRAINING FOR WORK UNDER A NEW DEAL PROGRAM

NATIONAL COUNCIL OF NEGRO WOMEN

Mary McLeod Bethune

BLACK VOTERS IN 1936

SCIENCE AND TECHNOLOGY

TECHNOLOGY AND WAR

Technological advancements from the 1930s became important tools during World War II and beyond. In 1934, physicist Enrico Fermi first split uranium atoms without realizing it. He had unknowingly discovered **nuclear fission**. Four years later, German scientists Otto Hahn and Lise Meitner demonstrated how to split uranium atoms in their laboratory. This experiment led to the development of **nuclear power** and the **atomic bomb**.

OTTO HAHN AND LISE MEITNER

Several countries, including the U.S, were actively developing radar technology. In 1935, British physicist Sir Robert Watson-Watt demonstrated a system for detecting aircraft using radio waves. It later became known as RADAR, which stands for Radio Detection and Ranging. Radar detection would soon become a key part of Britain's air defense during World War II.

SIR ROBERT WATSON-WATT WITH RADAR EQUIPMENT

The turbojet engine, invented in the 1930s, revolutionized the aviation industry. It allowed aircraft manufacturers to build bigger, faster, and more powerful airplanes. The world's first turbojet-powered plane, called the Heinkel He 178, flew on August 27, 1939, in Germany.

Aviation pioneer Igor Sikorsky designed and built the VS-300 helicopter in 1939. It took its first fight on September 14. The VS-300 was the world's first successful helicopter with a single three-blade rotor and a tail rotor. Single main rotors and smaller tail rotors are now standard in helicopter design.

IGOR SIKORSKY IN HIS VS-300 HELICOPTER

Heinkel He 178

SCIENTIFIC DISCOVERIES

The 1930s is known for other major breakthroughs. British mathematician Alan Turing made groundbreaking discoveries in computing. His work on **algorithms** and computation set the stage for the development of modern computers. Turing is also widely recognized as one of the key figures in the development of **artificial intelligence**.

The electron microscope, developed by Ernst Ruska and Max Knoll in 1931, was another groundbreaking invention. Its higher magnification and resolution allowed people to see extremely small things, such as viruses and cell structures, for the first time.

The decade saw the debut of other useful items. In 1930, a 3M engineer named Richard Drew invented Scotch tape. It was the world's first waterproof, clear sticky tape. The tape's original purpose was to seal food packages. People quickly began to use it for simple repairs. The handheld tape dispenser was introduced in 1939. A team of scientists at DuPont invented **synthetic** fiber nylon in 1935. It was first used to make hosiery. The first pairs of nylon stockings went on sale in Wilmington, Delaware, in 1939. Nylon would eventually be used to make other products, including parachutes, mosquito netting, and shoelaces!

CHOCOLATE CHIP COOKIE

INVENTOR:
Ruth Wakefield

YEAR INVENTED:
1938

EFFECT ON DAILY LIFE:
Now one of the most popular cookies in the U.S., the chocolate chip cookie was first made by Ruth Wakefield at the Toll House restaurant in Massachusetts.

DWARF PLANET

Astronomer Clyde Tombaugh discovered the dwarf planet Pluto on February 18, 1930, at the Lowell Observatory near Flagstaff, Arizona. Pluto was once considered the solar system's ninth planet but was reclassified as a dwarf planet in 2006.

Clyde Tombaugh

DAILY LIFE

LIFE IN THE '30s

The Great Depression had a huge impact on millions of people's daily lives. Many people lost their savings and were unable to afford housing. Houselessness became widespread. Many families sought shelter with relatives or moved to Hoovervilles. In larger cities, soup kitchens and breadlines provided free meals to people in need. Marriage and birth rates declined due to couples facing economic hardship. Desperate for work, many men turned to "riding the rails." They hopped on railroad cars in search of food, jobs, and shelter in other places.

People developed strategies to cope with the hard times. Homemakers kept gardens, canned food, and mended worn-out clothes to save on household expenses. Many women learned to make clothing out of cotton flour sacks. Flour companies even began printing sacks with colorful patterns to make them more attractive! Cooks stretched their food budgets with one-pot meals and casseroles. Friends gathered to play board games and cards rather than spending money on outside entertainment.

SOUP KITCHEN

"RIDING THE RAILS"

SCHOOL DAYS

High school graduation rates went up during the Great Depression. Job scarcity led many kids to stay in school. Parents also believed a high school education would improve their children's future job prospects.

1930s SLANG

Flivver

a car

LEAPIN' LIZARDS

Oh my goodness!

FASHION TRENDS

Joan Crawford

The showy fashions and boyish looks of the 1920s gave way to more practical, affordable styles during the 1930s. Women's dresses featured longer hemlines, slim waistlines, and flared skirts. Most women bought fewer clothes during the decade. They relied on hats, gloves, jewelry, and other accessories to add variety to their looks. Hollywood stars had a huge influence on fashion. They inspired the popularity of **bias-cut gowns**, fur accessories, and other glamorous trends. Many women wore padded shoulders and puffed sleeves made famous by actress Joan Crawford.

cloche-style hat

Men also aimed for both practicality and style during the Great Depression. Working-class men opted for simple, button-down shirts and flat caps. Men seeking a more stylish look often chose double-breasted suits, wide trousers, and neckties. Tennis player René Lacoste's polo shirt, featuring a crocodile logo, became a staple of men's sportswear. Hollywood also influenced men's fashion. Trench coats, worn by gangsters in movies, were popular. The pencil-thin mustache sported by actors Clark Gable, David Niven, and Vincent Price was another trend.

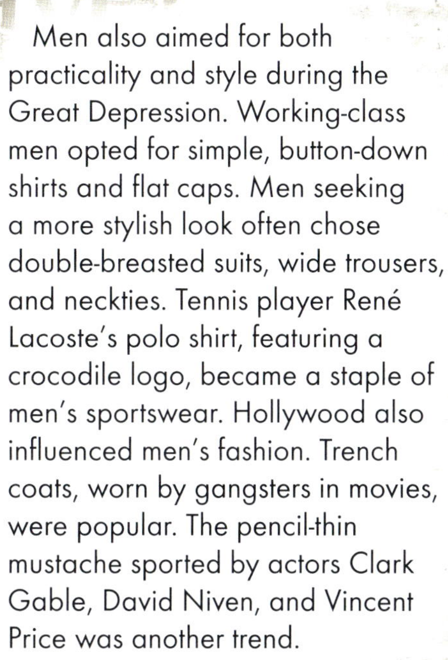

FUR ACCESSORIES

DOUBLE-BREASTED SUIT

TRENCH COATS

Clark Gable

PRODUCTS AND TOYS

Toys and games helped children and families cope with the hardships brought on by the Great Depression. Many families could no longer afford store-bought toys. Instead, they made their toys with materials they had on hand. Scrap wood provided material to make toy cars, blocks, and dollhouses. Kids cut dolls out of paper and dressed them in paper clothes.

SHIRLEY TEMPLE DOLL

Child actor Shirley Temple captured the hearts of millions during the 1930s. The Ideal Toy Company introduced the Shirley Temple doll in 1934. She had the actor's signature ringlets, dimpled smile, and matching clothes.

BALSA WOOD KITS

Balsa wood kits were an inexpensive and fun way for kids to build their own model gliders. Kits came with pieces of balsa, a lightweight wood, that fit together to form the fuselage, wings, and tail. A small piece of lead was also included to weight the nose.

VIEW MASTER

The View Master was introduced in 1939 at the World's Fair. It presents slides in 3D through a viewer. The first slides featured pictures of scenic attractions around the country. The View Master was originally intended for adults, but it eventually became a popular children's toy.

JIGSAW PUZZLES

Jigsaw puzzles rose in popularity during the 1930s. They were an inexpensive, reusable, and fun activity people could do together. By the early 1930s, improvements in cutting machine technology enabled the mass production of puzzles. Tens of millions of households enjoyed doing puzzles each week.

FINGER PAINTS

In 1931, Ruth Shaw invented a safe, nontoxic paint for children that she called finger paint. She believed finger paint could help children express themselves creatively and learn about art. By 1936, finger painting had become a popular activity in schools across the country.

BUCK ROGERS ROCKET PISTOL

The Buck Rogers rocket pistol was first sold in 1934. Its design was based on the weapon carried by a space-age comic strip character named Buck Rogers. The toy made a popping sound to match the rocket pistols seen in the comic strips.

BOARD GAMES

Board games were a popular form of cheap entertainment that families and friends could enjoy together. Monopoly, Scrabble, and Sorry! debuted during the decade and are still played today!

ARTS AND ENTERTAINMENT

PUBLICATIONS

The turmoil of the 1930s influenced many writers to explore themes of social unrest, poverty, and political concerns. John Steinbeck's stories often focused on people's struggles during the Great Depression. *The Grapes of Wrath*, published in 1939, won him the National Book Award and a Pulitzer Prize. It tells the story of a farm family that moves to California during the Dust Bowl. *Of Mice and Men*, published in 1937, is another Steinbeck masterpiece set during the Depression.

Reading was a favorite pastime for people of all ages. Detective fiction and mysteries provided a welcome escape from the troubles of the time. Agatha Christie's mystery novel *Murder on the Orient Express* was hugely popular. People's fascination with the future fueled interest in science fiction. Novels such as *Brave New World* by Aldous Huxley explored a future shaped by technology.

READING REC

TITLE:
THE HOBBIT

AUTHOR:
J.R.R. Tolkien

YEAR PUBLISHED:
1937

SUMMARY:
Hobbit Bilbo Baggins embarks on an adventure with a group of dwarves to reclaim their ancient home and treasure from the dragon Smaug, who has been hoarding it in the Lonely Mountain.

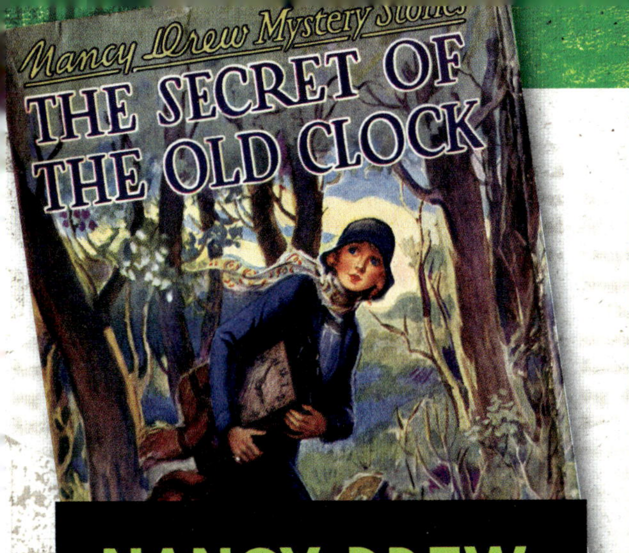

NANCY DREW

Teenage detective Nancy Drew made her debut in April 1930 in *The Secret of the Old Clock*. The book was the first in the beloved Nancy Drew mystery series. The original series would go on to include 56 books written by different authors under the pen name Carolyn Keene.

THEIR EYES WERE WATCHING GOD

Their Eyes Were Watching God is a 1937 novel written by Zora Neale Hurston. The novel, a southern love story featuring a Black woman named Janie, is applauded for its rich prose and unique characters. It is both Hurston's best-known work and among the most important novels to come out of the Harlem Renaissance.

THE GOOD EARTH

Pearl S. Buck achieved great success and a Pulitzer Prize with her novel *The Good Earth*, published in 1931. Its story follows the life of a man living in rural China in the early twentieth century. The novel was widely praised for accurately depicting traditional Chinese culture.

Superman

SUPERHERO SUPERSTARS

Detective Comics, later known as DC Comics, debuted in 1937. It featured stories about street crimes and detectives. Superman first appeared in 1938 in *Action Comics* #1. He was the world's first superhero with superhuman abilities. Batman debuted in 1939 in *Detective Comics* #27.

MOVIES

The 1930s are considered part of the Golden Age of Hollywood. A handful of movie studios controlled movie production, talent, and distribution. Movie theaters were often elegant places with plush seats, chandeliers, and ornate curtains. Millions of Americans went to the movies each week to be transported to exciting places far away from their daily struggles. **Genres** such as westerns, horror, and gangster movies were hugely popular. Movies typically opened with a newsreel, a preview, and a live-action short. Cartoons were also common. They introduced audiences to Mickey Mouse, Donald Duck, and other animated favorites!

Significant advancements in the film industry were made during the decade. Sound, camera, lighting, and other technologies continued to improve. The use of a color process called Technicolor became more common. Films looked and sounded better than ever!

The Wizard of Oz

AT THE BOX OFFICE

TOP-GROSSING FILMS OF THE 1930s

- ***Gone with the Wind*** **(1939)**
- ***Snow White and the Seven Dwarfs*** **(1937)**
- ***The Wizard of Oz*** **(1939)**
- ***Frankenstein*** **(1931)**
- ***Tom Sawyer*** **(1930)**
- ***King Kong*** **(1933)**
- ***Mr. Smith Goes to Washington*** **(1939)**
- ***Hell's Angels*** **(1930)**
- ***Cavalcade*** **(1933)**
- ***Saratoga*** **(1937)**

King Kong

SNOW WHITE AND THE SEVEN DWARFS

Snow White and the Seven Dwarfs debuted in 1937. It was Walt Disney's first feature-length animated film. Advanced sound and animation techniques brought the fairy tale to life. Songs such as "Someday My Prince Will Come" and "Heigh-Ho" would become classics. The movie was the highest-grossing film of 1938.

SHIRLEY TEMPLE

A charming child star named Shirley Temple was hugely popular during the 1930s. Her wholesome musicals cheered people up during the Depression. Her first hit movie was a 1934 musical called *Bright Eyes*. It featured Temple's signature song, "On the Good Ship Lollipop," and made her a box-office star!

KING KONG

The 1933 blockbuster movie *King Kong* introduced the world to the famous giant ape. It also made actor Fay Wray an international movie star! The filmmakers used miniatures, models, and **stop-motion animation** to bring the ape to life. These visual effects were groundbreaking at the time and would go on to become standard techniques in film production.

THE WIZARD OF OZ

The Wizard of Oz, released in 1939, delighted audiences with its imaginative story, memorable characters, and original songs. It is famous for using Technicolor to create the colorful Land of Oz. The movie won two Academy Awards and skyrocketed actor Judy Garland, who played Dorothy, to fame. It is one of the most beloved films of all time!

GONE WITH THE WIND

The 1939 movie *Gone with the Wind* is an epic historical romance set in the American South during the Civil War. It was based on the 1936 novel *Gone with the Wind* by Margaret Mitchell. The movie lasted four hours and included an intermission! The film won eight Academy Awards, including Best Picture. It remains one of the highest-grossing films of all time.

TELEVISION AND RADIO

The 1930s was the Golden Age of radio. It was one of the decade's most common sources of entertainment! Daytime programs entertained people in the afternoons. Kids enjoyed following the radio adventures of Flash Gordon, Buck Rogers, and other heroes after school. Families gathered around the radio in the evening to listen to programs everyone enjoyed.

Television technology advanced during the 1930s. Television sets went on sale late in the decade. They were expensive and had small screens. RCA made a splash with its television demonstration at the 1939 New York World's Fair. On April 30, 1939, RCA's National Broadcasting Company (NBC) launched regular television broadcasting. Its first telecast featured President Roosevelt dedicating the fair.

DAILY NEWS — NEW YORK'S PICTURE NEWSPAPER — FINAL

Daily---1,800,000 Sunday-3,150,000

Vol. 20. No. 109 — New York, Monday, October 31, 1938 — 48 Pages — 2 Cents

FAKE RADIO 'WAR' STIRS TERROR THROUGH U.S.

—Story on Page 2

"War" Victim

Caroline Castine, WPA actress, listening to this radio in West 45th St., heard announcement of "smoke in Times Square." Running to street, she fell, broke her arm.

"I Didn't Know". Orson Welles, after broadcast expresses amazement at public reaction. He adapted H. G. Wells' "War of the Worlds" for radio and played principal role. Left: a machine conceived for another H. G. Wells story. Dramatic description of landing of weird "machine from Mars" started last night's panic.

—Story on page 2.

WAR OF THE WORLDS BROADCAST

On October 30, 1938, the *Mercury Theatre on the Air* aired a dramatic radio presentation of the classic H.G. Wells novel *War of the Worlds*. The broadcast consisted of what sounded like a normal music program being interrupted by news bulletins. They described Martian armies invading Earth. Many listeners believed the bulletins were real and panicked!

AMOS 'N' ANDY

***Amos 'n' Andy* was a comedy series that featured white actors playing two Black characters named Amos Jones and Andy Brown. It became one of the most popular programs of the decade. However, its reliance on racial stereotypes caused great controversy shortly after the TV series aired in the early 1950s.**

The Guiding Light

SOAP OPERAS

Soap operas started during the 1930s. These daytime dramas were mainly aimed at female audiences. Their storylines often focused on the characters' romantic lives. The name "soap opera" emerged because the programs were often sponsored by companies that made soap and other household products. *The Guiding Light*, which started in 1937, became one of the longest-running soap operas in history.

THE SHADOW

The Shadow was a popular radio drama that featured a mysterious crime fighter called the Shadow. He had many gifts, including the ability to cloud people's minds to avoid being seen. The program opened with the lines, "Who knows what evil lurks in the hearts of men? The Shadow knows!" These lines are still recognized today!

THE LONE RANGER

The Lone Ranger was a radio program that began in 1933. It began airing on television in 1949. The show followed the adventures of a masked Texas Ranger and his Native American companion, Tonto, as they fought injustice in the west. The Lone Ranger rode a white stallion named Silver. The program was originally aimed at children, but it eventually drew a huge adult audience, too.

MUSIC

Music was a popular form of entertainment during the 1930s. It helped people find joy during difficult times. A New Deal program called the Federal Music Project funded music programs across the country. It offered free concerts to the public and led to the formation of new musical groups.

Radio broadcasts introduced audiences to a wide range of music. Jazz music, which became wildly popular during the 1920s, was still a fan favorite. An energetic style of jazz called swing dominated the 1930s. It inspired millions of people to kick up their heels on the dance floor! Swing music was made popular by big bands led by bandleaders such as Glenn Miller, Benny Goodman, and Duke Ellington.

ENDURANCE DANCES

Dance marathons started in the 1920s and had become a huge fad by the early 1930s. Couples would dance for days, weeks, or even months to win cash prizes. Dancers were disqualified when they stopped moving, so people learned to sleep while their partners held them up.

1930s PLAYLIST

- ***Minnie the Moocher*** **Cab Calloway (1931)**
- ***Brother, Can You Spare A Dime?*** **Bing Crosby (1932)**
- ***It Don't Mean a Thing (If It Ain't Got That Swing)*** **Duke Ellington (1932)**
- ***Cheek to Cheek*** **Fred Astaire (1935)**
- ***Sing, Sing, Sing (With a Swing)*** **Benny Goodman (1937)**
- ***A-Tisket, A-Tasket*** **Ella Fitzgerald (1938)**
- ***Over the Rainbow*** **Judy Garland (1939)**
- ***In The Mood*** **Glenn Miller (1939)**
- ***Strange Fruit*** **Billie Holiday (1939)**
- ***Back in the Saddle Again*** **Gene Autry (1939)**

JITTERBUG

The jitterbug is a type of swing dance. It incorporates moves from dances such as the Lindy Hop and the East Coast Swing. People often did the jitterbug to swing music played by big bands. The dance's lively moves often include hops, lifts, and twirls!

CROONERS

Crooners were singers who sang in a soft, soothing style. They were the first artists to use microphones during performances and recording sessions. While earlier singers had to project their voices, microphones let crooners sing more softly. Bing Crosby, Frank Sinatra, and Rudy Vallee were popular crooners during the 1930s.

Bing Crosby

ELLA FITZGERALD

Ella Fitzgerald was one of the most popular jazz singers of all time. She was known for her velvety voice, wide vocal range, and impressive scat singing. Fitzgerald's music career began when she entered talent shows in the early 1930s. In 1935, she made her first recording. Fitzgerald would go on to pack concert halls all over the world.

WOODY GUTHRIE

Woody Guthrie is one of the most popular and influential American folk singers to emerge from the Dust Bowl era. He is known for his folk ballads, children's songs, and songs about working class struggles. During the 1930s, Guthrie traveled to California with the Dust Bowl migrants, a journey that inspired many of his songs, including his best-known song "This Land Is Your Land."

Tex Ritter

COUNTRY AND WESTERN

Country artists such as Gene Autry, Tex Ritter, and Roy Rogers rose to fame during the 1930s as "singing cowboys" on records and in movies. They wore Stetson hats, cowboy boots, and western shirts and often sang about cowboys and the open range. Many yodeled or sang with a "twang." Dorothy Page was known as a "singing cowgirl."

U.S. SPORTS

Sports were a popular diversion for people during the Great Depression. Despite the hard times, radio broadcasts allowed fans to follow their favorite sporting events for free. Baseball continued to be a national favorite, with fans rooting for Babe Ruth, Lou Gehrig, and Joe DiMaggio.

Other sports were gaining popularity. Basketball held its first national collegiate tournament in 1939. Children started playing Little League baseball the same year. New swimming pools, tennis courts, gymnasiums, and golf courses were built through New Deal programs. They helped to increase participation in sports in communities across the country.

MVP

NAME: BABE DIDRIKSON ZAHARIAS

SPORTS:
golf, basketball, baseball, track and field, and other sports

TEAMS:
Golden Cyclones basketball team from 1929 to 1932

YEARS ACTIVE:
early 1930s until her death in 1956

KNOWN FOR:
An American athlete who excelled in every sport she tried, Didrikson earned the nickname "Babe" for her baseball hitting abilities, won two gold medals and a silver in track and field at the 1932 Summer Olympics, and later took up golf, going on to win 10 LPGA championships.

CALLED SHOT

New York Yankee Babe Ruth made history when he seemingly "called" a home run while facing the Chicago Cubs during the 1932 World Series. After taking two strikes, Ruth pointed two fingers toward center field. On the next pitch, he hit a home run that landed in the deepest part of the center field bleachers. The jersey that Ruth wore that day was later sold for more than $24 million!

JOHNNY WEISSMULLER

Johnny Weissmuller was an American swimmer and actor. He achieved great success in swimming during the 1920s and early 1930s. He won five Olympic gold medals and set 67 world records. He was the first man to swim the 100-meter freestyle in under one minute. After his swimming career ended, he became famous for playing Tarzan in a series of films.

SEABISCUIT

Seabiscuit was a racehorse who captivated the public's attention during the 1930s. Seabiscuit started as a mistreated underdog. He only won 5 of his first 35 races, and he often finished near the back of the field. A new coach helped Seabiscuit achieve success. His triumph against champion racer War Admiral in 1938 made Seabiscuit a symbol of hope during the Depression.

JOE LOUIS

Joe Louis was among the most famous boxers of the 1930s. He won the heavyweight boxing championship in 1937 by defeating James J. Braddock. This victory marked the beginning of Louis's reign as the world heavyweight champion, a title he held for nearly 12 years. His victory over German Max Schmeling in 1938 became a symbol of America's triumph over Nazi Germany.

LOU GEHRIG

Lou Gehrig was a baseball great for the New York Yankees. He was known for his hitting skills and humble nature. He played 2,130 games in a row over 14 years, a streak that earned him the nickname "The Iron Horse." Gehrig retired in 1939 when he was diagnosed with amyotrophic lateral sclerosis, also known as ALS or Lou Gehrig's disease.

GLOBAL SPORTS

The Great Depression had a strong grip on international sports. People across the globe found inexpensive ways to enjoy sports and recreation. Cycling was popular in France while the Nordic countries embraced skiing. English soccer players had their wages capped through the decade, which kept ticket prices low. Because of this, fans packed soccer matches despite the economic hardships many of them endured.

The decade's Olympic Games also helped raise people's spirits. The Summer Games of 1936 held in Berlin, Germany, had extra importance. Black athletes from the U.S. undermined Adolf Hitler's racist ideas with triumphant wins!

OLYMPICS OF THE 1930s

WINTER 1932
LAKE PLACID, NEW YORK, U.S.

WINTER 1936
GARMISCH-PARTENKIRCHEN, GERMANY

SUMMER 1936
BERLIN, GERMANY

SUMMER 1932
LOS ANGELES, CALIFORNIA, U.S.

Jesse Owens

DON BRADMAN

Australian Don Bradman is regarded as one of cricket's greatest batsmen and run scorers of all time. In 1930, he achieved a score of 334 runs in one innings during a Test match against England. This feat made him a cricket legend!

1936 SUMMER OLYMPICS IN BERLIN

The 1936 Summer Olympics were hosted in Berlin, Germany. Adolf Hitler used these Games to falsely present Germany as a peaceful and tolerant nation. He also wanted to confirm his racist ideas by having Germans dominate the Games. However, victories by multiple Black athletes, including Jesse Owens, Cornelius Johnson, and Ralph Metcalfe, proved Hitler wrong.

FIFA WORLD CUP

The inaugural FIFA World Cup took place in Uruguay in 1930. Thirteen teams entered the tournament, including a team from the U.S. Uruguay emerged as the champion by defeating Argentina 4–2 in the final.

SUMMER OLYMPICS IN LOS ANGELES

The 1932 Summer Olympics were hosted in Los Angeles, California. Around 100,000 people attended the opening ceremony. The Games featured notable performances by U.S. athlete Babe Didrikson in track and field and Japanese teenager Kusuo Kitamura in swimming.

TIMELINE

FEBRUARY 18, 1930
Astronomer Clyde Tombaugh discovers the dwarf planet Pluto

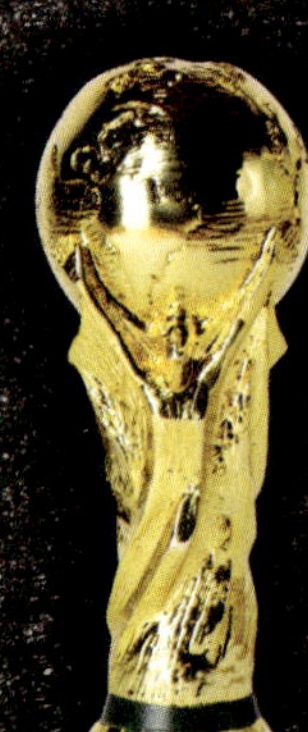

JULY 13 TO 30, 1930
The first FIFA World Cup takes place in Uruguay

JUNE 17, 1930
President Herbert Hoover signs the Smoot-Hawley Tariff Act

1931
The electron microscope is invented

MARCH 3, 1931
"The Star-Spangled Banner" becomes the official U.S. national anthem

MAY 1, 1931
The Empire State Building opens in New York City

OCTOBER 1, 1932
Babe Ruth appears to call his home run during the World Series

NOVEMBER 8, 1932
Franklin D. Roosevelt wins his first presidential election

MARCH 22, 1933
Prisoners arrive at the first concentration camp, Dachau, in Nazi Germany

JANUARY 30, 1933
The first episode of *The Lone Ranger* radio program airs

AUGUST 2, 1934
Adolf Hitler becomes dictator of Germany

DECEMBER 28, 1934
The musical *Bright Eyes* starring Shirley Temple is released in theaters

MARCH 1933
Around 15 million people are unemployed in the U.S.

APRIL 7, 1933
***King Kong* is released in theaters**

OCTOBER 1934
Physicist Enrico Fermi splits uranium atoms

APRIL 14, 1935
Black Sunday, one of the worst dust storms in American history, blasts the Great Plains

AUGUST 9, 1936
Jesse Owens wins his fourth gold medal at the Berlin Olympics

JANUARY 1937
The first payments into Social Security are made

NOVEMBER 5, 1935
Parker Brothers releases the board game Monopoly

JULY 17, 1936
General Francisco Franco begins the Spanish Civil War

MAY 6, 1937
The *Hindenburg* explodes over New Jersey

MAY 6, 1935
President Roosevelt signs the order forming the Works Progress Administration

NOVEMBER 3, 1936
Roosevelt is reelected president

JULY 2, 1937
Amelia Earhart disappears while on a flight around the world

OCTOBER 30, 1938
The radio broadcast of *War of the Worlds* sends some listeners into a panic

SEPTEMBER 1, 1939
Hitler's troops invade Poland, starting World War II

APRIL 30, 1939
RCA demonstrates the television at the New York World's Fair

JUNE 1938
Superman is introduced in *Action Comics* #1

NOVEMBER 9, 1938
Violence against German Jews erupts into *Kristallnacht*

AUGUST 25, 1939
The film *The Wizard of Oz* is released

GLOSSARY

algorithms—sets of instructions given to computer programs to solve specific problems

appeasement—giving someone what they want to avoid a conflict

artificial intelligence—a computer's ability to do things a human mind can do

atomic bomb—a bomb that releases nuclear energy to cause destruction

authoritarianism—a type of leadership where a government has all the power and people do not have many choices or freedoms

bias-cut gowns—dresses where fabric is cut diagonally instead of straight across the grain, allowing the fabric to flow more naturally

genres—categories of a kind of art based on style, form, or content

Great Depression—a time in world history when many countries experienced economic crisis; the Great Depression began in 1929 and lasted through the 1930s.

Harlem Renaissance—a movement of artistic and cultural expression by Black Americans in Harlem, New York, during the early 1900s

labor unions—organizations of workers who come together to get fair treatment, good working conditions, and ensure other workers' rights

nonaggression pact—a treaty between two or more states agreeing not to engage in military action against each other

nuclear fission—a process in which the nucleus of an atom splits into two or more parts

nuclear power—energy created by splitting apart the nuclei of atoms

racial stereotypes—unfair and oversimplified beliefs about a group of people based on their race

scat—a type of jazz singing that uses made-up words and melodies, usually while improvising

squalor—very dirty, unpleasant conditions

stop-motion animation—a filming technique that involves taking a series of photographs of an object and making small adjustments to its position or appearance between each shot; when the photos are played back quickly, the object appears to be moving.

synthetic—related to something that is made by people using chemicals

tariff—a tax on goods that are brought into a country from another country

Treaty of Versailles—a formal peace treaty signed on June 28, 1919, that officially ended World War I between Germany and the Allied Powers

WRITE ABOUT IT!

- What do you think were the most important moments during the 1930s? **Why?**

- Which part of the 1930s would you have liked to experience? **Why?**

- Are there any events from the 1930s that you think affect life today? **What are they?**

ALSO CHECK OUT

INDEX

The images in this book are reproduced through the courtesy of: Archive PL/ Alamy Stock Photo, front cover (Roosevelt), p. 11 (Roosevelt); rangizzz, front cover (cookie); PictureLux/ The Hollywood Archive/ Alamy Stock Photo, front cover (Louis); Dorothea Lange/ Wikipedia, front cover (mother); Moviestore Collection Ltd/ Alamy Stock Photo, front cover (The Wizard of Oz); CBW/ Alamy Stock Photo, front cover (The Hobbit), p. 20 (Hahn and Meitner); Glasshouse Images/ Alamy Stock Photo, front cover (dancing); World History Archive/ Alamy Stock Photo, pp. 3 (Hindenburg), 8 (Hooverville), 9 (Hindenburg), 14 (protesters), 15 (Franco), 32 (The Wizard of Oz); Bettmann/ Contributor/ Getty Images, pp. 3 (Roosevelt), 6, 13 (Roosevelt, all), 18, 19 (voters), 21 (Sikorsky), 27 (coats), 33 (Gone with the Wind), 37 (Ritter), 43 (March 1933), 44 (Roosevelt), 45 (July 1937); ARCHIVIO GBB/ Alamy Stock Photo, pp. 3 (Gable), 27 (Gable); Everett Collection Inc/ Alamy Stock Photo, pp. 3 (Fitzgerald), 19 (New Deal), 37 (Fitzgerald); History and Art Collection/ Alamy Stock Photo, p. 4 (shoes); fstop123, p. 4 (radio); Minnesota Historical Society/ Contributor/ Getty Images, p. 4 (child); Mirrorpix/ Contributor/ Getty Images, p. 5 (mending); Smith Archive/ Alamy Stock Photo, pp. 5 (swimming), 11 (demonstrators); Winai Tepsuttinun, p. 7 (gas); Scukrov, p. 7 (milk); Photo Builder, p. 7 (newspaper); phive2015, p. 7 (bread); Steve Cukrov, p. 7 (Hershey); National Archives at College Park/ Wikipedia, p. 8 (Empire State Building); Harris & Ewing/ Wikipedia, p. 8 (Earhart); Penta Springs Limited/ Alamy Stock Photo, p. 9 (refugees); Historic Illustrations/ Alamy Stock Photo, p. 9 (bridge); IanDagnall Computing/ Alamy Stock Photo, p. 10; Everett Collection Historical/ Alamy Stock Photo, pp. 11 (voting), 17 (newspapers), 38; Album/ Alamy Stock Photo, p. 14 (García); Photo 12/ Alamy Stock Photo, pp. 14 (soldiers), 34; Chronicle/ Alamy Stock Photo, pp. 14 (troops), 40 (Winter 1932); Heritage Image Partnership Ltd/ Alamy Stock Photo, pp. 15 (Kristallnacht), 29 (puzzle); Shawshots/ Alamy Stock Photo, p. 17 (Poland); Historical/ Contributor/ Getty Images, pp. 17 (Hitler), 43 (Hitler); Jonathan Park, p. 17 (flag); Universal History Archive/ Contributor/ Getty Images, p. 19 (Bethune); Afro Newspaper/ Gado/ Contributor/ Getty Images, p. 19 (National Council of Negro Women); Science & Society Picture Library/ Contributor/ Getty Images, p. 20 (Watson-Watt); Vintage Mechanics/ Alamy Stock Photo, p. 21 (Heinkel He 178); Space Priest, p. 22 (cookies); INTERFOTO/ Alamy Stock Photo, pp. 22 (Wakefield), 31 (Neale), 40 (Summer 1932); NASA/ Johns Hopkins University Applied Physics Laboratory/ Southwest Research Institute, p. 23 (Pluto); GL Archive/ Alamy Stock Photo, p. 23 (Tombaugh); Rolls Press/ Popperfoto/ Contributor/ Getty Images, p. 24 (soup kitchen); ClassicStock/ Alamy Stock Photo, pp. 24 ("riding the rails"), 27 (suit); Sueddeutsche Zeitung Photo/ Alamy Stock Photo, p. 26 (hat); LETTY LYNTON/ Everett Collection, p. 26 (Crawford); Camerique/ Contributor/ Getty Images, p. 27 (fur); Norgal | Dreamstime.com, p. 28 (Balsa); RLPM Collection/ Alamy Stock Photo, p. 28 (doll); Bill Truran/ Alamy Stock Photo, p. 29 (View Master); Alona_S, p. 29 (paint); antefixus21/ Flickr, p. 29 (pistol); JOHN GOMEZ, p. 29 (Monopoly); David Pimborough/ Alamy Stock Photo, p. 30; Russell H. Tandy/ Wikipedia, p. 31 (Drew); Pictorial Press Ltd/ Alamy Stock Photo, pp. 31 (Superman), 37 (Crosby); Masheter Movie Archive/ Alamy Stock Photo, p. 32 (King Kong); Allstar Picture Library Limited./ Alamy Stock Photo, pp. 33 (Snow White), 45 (August 1939); Entertainment Pictures/ Alamy Stock Photo, p. 33 (Temple); C.B.S. Radio/ Everett Collection, p. 35 (The Guiding Light); Bill Waterson/ Alamy Stock Photo, p. 35 (Shadow); RGR Collection/ Alamy Stock Photo, p. 35 (Lone Ranger); Heritage Images/ Contributor/ Getty Images, p. 36; Transcendental Graphics/ Contributor/ Getty Images, p. 39 (Ruth); Joseph W. Brady/ ASSOCIATED PRESS/ AP Newsroom, p. 39 (Louis); AP/ ASSOCIATED PRESS/ AP Newsroom, p. 39 (Gehrig); Michelle Bridges/ Alamy Stock Photo, p. 40 (Summer 1936); Hi-Story/ Alamy Stock Photo, p. 40 (Winter 1936); The Print Collector/ Alamy Stock Photo, p. 41 (Owens); Ken Kelly/ Popperfoto/ Contributor/ Getty Images, p. 41 (Bradman); Popperfoto/ Contributor/ Getty Images, p. 41 (FIFA); Nikolay N. Antonov, p. 42 (July 1930); Underwood & Underwood/ Wikipedia, p. 42 (June 1930); Kristina Blokhin/ Alamy Stock Photo, p. 42 (May 1931); PictureLake, p. 43 (October 1934); ullstein bild Dtl./ Contributor/ Getty Images, p. 44 (August 1936); lorenzc/ IMGBIN, p. 45 (June 1938).